HOW TO STOP LIKE SH

SNAP OUT OF IT GEEZ

LET THE WHINING STOP RIGHT NOW AND START LIVING

Clarke Wickens

Table of Contents

PART 1

Chapter 1:

Your Motivational Partner In Life

We all have friends. We all have parents. We may have a partner or other half. We all have teachers.

We love and respect all of them and hopefully, they do too. But have we ever wondered why we do that?

Why do we have to love someone who brought us into this world? Why do we love a person who is not related to us whatsoever, but has a connection with us, and hence we like to hang around them? Why do we respect someone who is being paid to do what makes him respectable?

The answer to all these is simple. They make us a better version of ourselves. Without these people in our lives, we won't be as good as we are right now.

It doesn't matter where we stand right now in our lives, there would always be someone backing you up whenever you feel low.

People tend to seek loneliness and a quiet corner whenever life hits hard. But what they don't realize is that there are people in their lives who have a duty towards you.

Either that be your parents or friends or partner or anyone for that case, you need to find time to give them a chance to show their true affections towards you. You need to give them

Your parents can't give up on you because you are a part of them. You have their legacy to keep and spread. They want you to be a better person than they ever were, hence they will always support you no matter what the world does to you.

Your friends have a bond of loyalty towards you which is the basic root of any friendship. They will always try to help you get up no matter how many times you fall.

All these people owe you this support. And you owe it to them to be a source of inspiration when they want a shoulder to cry. When they want a person to listen and feel their pain. When they need someone to be able to share some time with them without a grain of self-interest.

These things make us stronger as a human and make us grow and evolve as a Specie.

You can find motivation and inspiration from anyone. It may even be a guard in your office or a worker in your office who you might see once a week.

Basic human nature makes us susceptible to the need of finding company. It doesn't matter where it comes from. What you need is a person who can devote a selfless minute of his or her life to you and feels good when they realize they have made a positive change in your life.

Everyone goes through this phase of loneliness but we always find a person who makes us the most comfortable.

The person who reimburses our self-belief. The person who makes us take one more try, one more chance, not for us but for them too. This person is your true motivational partner in life.

Chapter 2:

Who Are You Working For?

Who you work for is up to you,

but ultimately every person has a choice in that decision.

Whether you are self-employed, self-made, or salaried,

You determine your own destiny.

As Earl Nightingale said, only the successful will admit it.

You might work for one company your whole life,

but ultimately you are still working for yourself and your family.

If you do not like the practices of your company,

you have the power to leave and make a change.

You must choose to serve who you believe to be worthy of your life.

High self-esteem stops successful people ever feeling subordinate to anyone.

Achieve your goals by envisioning yourself providing quality service in the companies and places that will maximise your chances of success.

Always view yourself as equal to everybody.

All of us have unique talents and qualities within us.

Acknowledg that we can learn from anybody.

Nobody is above or below us.

You can build such qualities that are keys to success.

If one client is taking all your time, reassess his or her value.

If the contract is no longer rewarding, end it as soon as possible.

Doesn't matter if it is a business or personal relationship.

You must get clear on the fact that you are working for you.

You should consider no one your boss.

You should view whoever pays you as a client,

As such you should provide them the best service you can.

Always look to create more opportunity for your business.

Don't look for security - it doesn't exist.

Even if you find it for a time, I guarantee it will be boring at best.

Look for productivity and progression.

Change is definite. It is the only constant.

It will be up to you whether it is progression or regression.

Work with people who have similar goals and objectives.

You should always work with, never for.

Remember that you are always working for yourself.

If working with a company is not bringing you any closer to your goal,

End it now and find one that will.

You should never feel stuck in a job because leaving it is only a letter or phone call away.

You can replace that income in a million different ways.

If you don't like someone scheduling your week for you, start your own business.

If you don't know how, get the training.

Investing in your skills is an investment in your future.

Learning doesn't end with high school.

That was only the beginning – that was practice

Be a life-long learner.

Learn on the job.

Learn so you can achieve more.

Once you admit that you are working for you,
change your bosses title to 'client'.
Open your eyes to a world of other big and wonderful opportunities.

Realize that you are more valuable than you previously believed yourself to be.
Believe you will are incredibly valuable, and you deserve to be paid accordingly.

Whether you are a minimum wage worker or a company director,
you probably haven't even scratched the surface of your capabilities.

Every time someone places limits on what is possible, somebody proves them wrong.
You work for yourself, the possibilities are limitless.

Chapter 3:

What To Do When You Feel Like Your Work is not Good Enough

Feeling like your work is not good enough is very common; your nerves can get better of you at any time throughout your professional life. There is nothing wrong with nerves; It tells you that you care about improving and doing well. Unfortunately, too much nervousness can lead to major self-doubt, and that can be crippling. You are probably very good at your work, and when even once you take a dip, you think that things are not like how they seem to you. If this is something you're feeling, then you're not alone, and this thing is known as Imposter Syndrome. This term is used to describe self-doubt and inadequacy. This one thing leaves people fearing that there might be someone who will expose them. The more pressure you apply to yourself, the more dislocation is likely to occur. You create more anxiety, which creates more fear, which creates more self-doubt. You don't have to continue like this. You can counter it.

Beyond Work

If your imposter syndrome affects you at work, you should take some time out and start focusing on other areas of your life. There are chances that there is something in your personal life that is hindering your work life. This could be anything your sleep routine, friends, diet, or even your relationships. There is a host of external factors that can affect your performance. If there are some boxes you aren't ticking, then there is a high chance of you not performing well at work.

You're Better Than You Think

When you're being crippled by self-doubt, the first thing you have to think about is why you were hired in the first place. The interviewers saw something in you that they believed would improve the business.

So, do you think they would recruit someone who can't do the job? No, they saw your talent, they saw something in you, and you will come good.

When you find yourself in this position, take a moment to write down a few things that you believe led to you being in the role you are now. What did those recruiters see? What did your boss recognize in you? You can also look back on a period of time where you were clicking and felt victorious. What was different then versus now? Was there an external issue like diet, exercise, socializing, etc.?

Check Yourself Before You Wreck Yourself

A checklist might be of some use to you. If you have a list to measure yourself against, then it gives you more than just one thing to judge yourself against. We're far too quick to doubt ourselves and criticize harshly.

The most obvious checklist in terms of work is technical or hard skills, but soft skills matter, too. It's also important to remember that while you're technically proficient now, things move quickly, and you'll reach a point where everything changes, and you have to keep up. You might not ever excel at something, but you can accept the change and adapt to the best of your ability.

It matters that you're hard-working, loyal, honest, and trustworthy. There's more to judge yourself on than just your job. Even if you make a mistake, it's temporary, and you can fix it.

Do you take criticism well? Are you teachable? Easy to coach? Soft skills count for something, which you can look to even at your lowest point and recognize you have strengths.

When you're struggling through a day, week, or even a month, take one large step backward and think about what it is you're unhappy with. What's causing your unhappiness, and how can you improve it?

It comes down to how well you know yourself. If you're clear on what your values are and what you want out of life, then you're going to be fine. If the organization you work for can't respect your values and harness your strengths, then you're better off elsewhere. So, it is extremely important to take time out for that self check-in there could be times you talk to yourself in negative light. Checking in with yourself regularly and not feeding yourself negativity could be one-step forward

Chapter 4:

Visualise Your Success In Life

When you have a clear idea of what you want in life, it becomes easier to achieve somehow. When you visualize yourself doing something, you automatically tend to get the results better. You can imagine your success in your mind before you even reach it so that it gives you a sense of comfort. You get the confidence that you can do whatever you desire. You complete your task more quickly because you have already done it once in your mind before even starting it. It relaxes us so we can interpret the outcome. You dream about your goals and remind yourself almost every day what you genuinely want or need. You become goal-oriented just by imagining your outcomes and results. Your brain tends to provide you with every possible option of opportunity you can have by visualizing. By this, you can take your dreams and desire into the real world and achieve them by knowing the possible outcome already.

Everyone today wants their picture-perfect life. They are derived from working for it, and they even manage to achieve it sometimes. People love the success which they had already estimated to happen one day. They knew they would be successful because they not only worked for it but, they also visualized it in their brains. Everything eventually falls into place once you remind yourself of your goals constantly and sometimes write it into a few words. Writing your goals down helps you immensely. It is the idea of a constant reminder for you. So, now whenever you look on that paper or note, you find yourself recognizing your path towards success. That is one of the ways you could visualize yourself as a successful person in the coming era.

Another way to visualize your success is through private dialogue. One has to talk its way through success. It's a meaningful way to know your heart's content and what it is you are looking for in this whole dilemma. You can then easily interpret your thoughts into words. It becomes easier to tell people what you want. It is an essential factor to choose between something. Weighing your options, analyzing every detail, and you get your answer. It requires planning for every big event ahead and those to come. You ready yourself for such things beforehand so that you will know the result.

Every single goal of yours will count. So, we have to make sure that we give our attention to short-term goals and long-term goals. We have to take in the details, not leaving anything behind in the way or so. We have to make sure that everything we do is considered by ourselves first. Short-term goals are necessary for you to achieve small incomes, giving you a sense of pride. Long-term plans are more time-consuming, and it takes a lot of hard work and patience from a person. Visualizing a long-term goal might be a risk, something as big as a long-term achievement can have loads of different outcomes, and we may get distracted from our goal to become successful in life. But, visualizing does help you work correctly to get to know what will be your next step. You can make schemes in your mind about specific projects and how to work them out. Those scheming will help you in your present and future. So, it is essential to look at every small detail and imagine short-term goals and long-term goals.

Visualizing your success creates creative ideas in your mind. Your mind gets used to imagining things like these, and it automatically processes the whole plan in your mind. You then start to get more ideas and opportunities in life. You just need to close your eyes and imagine whatever you need to in as vivid detail as possible. Almost everything done by you is a result of thoughts of your mind. It is like another person living inside of you, who tells you what to do. It asks you to be alert and move. It also means the result of the possible outcome of a situation. Every action of you is your mind. Every word you speak is your mind talking.

Chapter 5:

Understanding Yourself

Today we're going to talk about a topic that hopefully helps you become more aware of who you are as a person. And why do you exist right here and right now on this Earth. Because if we don't know who we are, if we don't understand ourselves, then how can we expect to other stand and relate to others? And why we even matter?

How many of you think that you can describe yourself accurately? If someone were to ask you exactly who you are, what would you say? Most of us would say we are Teachers, doctors, lawyers, etc. We would associate our lives with our profession.

But is that really what we are really all about?

Today I want to ask you not what you do, and not let your career define you, but rather what makes you feel truly alive and connected with the world? What is it about your profession that made you want to dedicated your life and time to it? Is there something about the job that makes you want to get up everyday and show up for the work, or is it merely to collect the paycheck at the end of the month?

I believe that that there is something in each and everyone of us that makes us who we are, and keeps us truly alive and full. For those that dedicate their lives to be Teachers, maybe they see themselves as an educator, a role model, a person who is in charge of helping a kid grow up, a nurturer, a parental figure. For Doctors, maybe they see themselves as healers, as someone who feels passionate about bringing life to someone. Whatever it may be, there is more to them than their careers.

For me, I see myself as a future caregiver, and to enrich the lives of my family members. That is something that I feel is one of my purpose in life. That I was born, not to provide for my family monetary per se, but to provide the care and support for them in their old age. That is one of my primary objectives. Otherwise, I see and understand myself as a person who loves to share knowledge with others, as I am doing right now. I love to help others in some way of form, either to inspire them, to lift their spirits, or to just be there for them when they need a crying shoulder. I love to help others fulfill their greatest potential, and it fills my heart with joy knowing that someone has benefitted from my advice. From what I have to say. And that what i have to say actually does hold some merit, some substance, and it is helping the lives of someone out there.. to help them make better decisions, and to help the, realise that life is truly wonderful. That is who i am.

Whenever I try to do something outside of that sphere, when what I do does not help someone in some way or another, I feel a sense of dread. I feel that what I do becomes misaligned with my calling, and I drag my feet each day to get those tasks done. That is something that I have realized about myself. And it might be happening to you too.

If u do not know exactly who you are and why you are here on this Earth, i highly encourage you to take the time to go on a self-discovery journey, however long it may take, to figure that out. Only when you know exactly who you are, can you start doing the work that aligns with ur purpose and calling. I don't meant this is in a religious way, but i believe that each and every one of us are here for a reason, whether it may to serve others, to help your fellow human beings, or to share your talents with the world, we should all be doing something with our lives that is at least close to that, if not exactly that.

So I challenge each and everyone of you to take this seriously because I believe you will be much happier for it. Start aligning your work with your purpose and you will find that life is truly worth living.

Chapter 6:

10 Habits That Can Ruin Your Day

Habits are the building blocks of our day. No matter how you spin it, either way, every detail matters.

The little actionable habits eventually sets you up to a either having a fulfilling day, or one that you have just totally wasted away. Nothing is as bad as destructive habits as they sabotage your daily productivity. Slowly, you slip further and further until it's too late when you've realized the damage that they have done to your life.

Bad habits are insidious! They drag down your life, lowers down your levels of accuracy, and make your performance less creative and stifling. It is essential, not only for productivity, to gain control of your bad habits. AS Grenville Kleiser once noted, "Constant self-discipline and self-control help you develop greatness of character." Nonetheless, it is important to stop and ask: what do you need today to get rid of or change? Sure, you can add or adjust new skills into your daily life.

Below are ten persistent habits that can ruin your day's success and productivity.

1. Hitting The Snooze Button.

Your mind, while you sleep, moves through a comprehensive series of cycles, the last one alerting you to wake up. While you crave for ten more minutes of sleep as the alarm goes off, what do you do? You whacked the snooze button. We're all guilty of this! If you don't suck it up, rip off the cover and start your morning, the rest of your day will be flawed. How do you expect your day to be strong once you don't start it off strong? You will feel far more optimistic, strong and fully prepared when you wake up without hitting the snooze button. So avoid the snooze button at any cost if you want a productive day ahead!

2. Wasting Your "Getting Ready" Hours.

You might need to reconsider the scrolling of Instagram and Facebook or the inane program you put on behind the scenes while preparing. These things have a time and place to partake in them – for example when you've accomplished your day's work and need some time to unwind and relax; however the time isn't now. Your morning schedule ought to be an interaction that prepares and energizes you for the day ahead. The objective is to accomplish something that animates your mind within the first hour of being conscious, so you can be more inventive, invigorated, gainful, and connected with all through the entire day! Avoiding this sweeps you away from normalizing the worst habit you might have: distraction. Instead, give yourself a chance to breathe the fine morning, anticipate the day's wonder and be thankful for whatever you have.

3. Failing To Prioritize Your Breakfast.

Energizing your day is essential if you wish for a very productive day. Energizing your body system requires that you prioritize eating your breakfast. However, the contents of your breakfast must entail something that will ensure that your day is not slowed down by noon. This means a blend of high - fiber foods such as proteins and healthy must be incorporated. Avoid taking too many sugars and heavy starches. The goal is to satiate and energize your body for the day.

4. Ruminating on the Problems of Yesterday And Negativity.

Don't take yesterday's problems to your new day if you want to start your day off right. If the day before you had difficult meetings and talks and you woke up ruminating about your horrific experiences, leave that negativity at your doorway. Moreover, if the problem you are lamenting about have been solved, then you shouldn't dwell on the past. Research suggests that we usually encounter more positive than negative events in a day. Still, often your mind concentrates on the negative due to a subconscious distortion called the negative distortion. By choosing not to focus on negative events and thinking about what's going well, you can learn to take advantage of the strength of the positive events around us. Raising negativity only increases stress. Let go of it and get on without it!

5. Leaving Your Day To Randomness.

Do not let stuff just simply happen to you; do it. Failure to create a structured day leads to a totally random day. A random day lacking direction, focus, and efficiency. Distractions will also creep into your day more readily because you have allowed randomness to happen to you. Instead, have a clear and precise list of what you need to focus for the day. This serves as a framework and a boundary for you to work within. Another thing you should consider is to spend your first 90 minutes on the most thoughtful and important task for the day. This allows you to know the big things out right at the beginning, reducing your cognitive burden for the rest of the day.

6. Becoming Involved With the Overview.

How frequently have you woken up, and before you can stretch and grin, you groan pretty much all the have-to for now and the fragmented musts from yesterday? This unhealthy habit will ruin your great day ahead. Know and understand these are simply contemplations. You can decide to recalibrate by pondering all you must be thankful for and searching for the splendid focuses in your day. Shift thinking, and you'll begin the day empowered.

7. Overscheduling and Over-Engagement.

People tend to underestimate how long things take with so many things to do. This habit of overscheduling and over-engagement can quickly lead to burn out. Always ensure that you permit extra time and energy for the unforeseen. Take regular breaks and don't overcommit to other people. This gives you more freedom for yourself and you won't be running the risk of letting others down by not turning up. Try not to overestimate what you can complete, so you won't feel like a disappointment. Be sensible and practical with your scheduling. Unexpectedly and eventually, you'll complete more.

8. Postponing or Discarding the Tough Tasks.

We have a restricted measure of mental energy, and as we exhaust this energy, our dynamic and efficiency decrease quickly. This is called decision exhaustion. Running the bad habit of postponing and disregarding the tough tasks will trigger this reaction in us. At the point when you put off extreme assignments till late in the day because they're scary, you deplete more and more of your mental resources. To beat choice weariness, you should handle complex assignments toward the beginning of the day when your brain is new.

9. Failure To Prioritize Your Self-Care.

Work, family commitments, and generally talking of the general obligations give almost everyone an awesome excuse to let your self-care rehearses pass by the wayside. Achievement-oriented minds of individuals see how basic self-care is to their expert achievement. Invest energy doing things that bring you delight and backing your psychological and actual wellbeing. "Success" doesn't exclusively apply to your finances or expert accomplishments.

10. Waiting for the Easier Way Out / Waiting for the Perfect Hack of Your Life.

The most noticeably awful everyday habit is trusting that things will occur and for a chance to thump at your entryway. As such, you become an inactive onlooker, not a proactive part of your own life. Once in a while, it shows itself as the quest for simple little-known techniques. Rather than getting down to work, ineffective individuals search how to take care of job quicker for quite a long time. Try not to begin with a #lifehack search on the internet unless it really does improve your productivity without sacrificing the necessary steps you need to take each day to achieve holistic success

✓ Merging It All Together

A portion of these habits may appear to be minor, yet they add up. Most amount to an individual decision between immediate pleasures and enduring ones. The most exceedingly awful propensity is forgetting about what matters to you. Always remember that you are just one habit away from changing you life forever.

Snap Out of It Geez

Chapter 7:

Stop Lying To Yourself

What do you think you are doing with your life? What do you keep on telling everyone you are up to? What ambitions do you make for yourself? What ideas do you follow? What goals do you want to follow and do you really have no choice in any of these?

These are not some random rude questions one might ask you. Because you deserve all of them if you still don't have anything meaningful in your life to stand behind.

You need to find a real achievement in your life that can make you feel accomplished.

Life is always a hard race to finish line with all of us running for the same goal of glory and success. But not all of us have the thing that will get us to that line first. SO when we fail to get there, we make reasons for our failure.

The reality is that it is never OK to make excuses for your failure when you weren't even eligible to join others to start with.

You have been lying to yourself this whole time, telling yourself that you have everything that takes to beat everyone to that finish line!

You have been lying to yourself saying that you are better than anyone there who came well prepared!

You keep telling yourself that you have a better understanding of things that you have just seen in your life for the first time! That you have a better approach towards life. That you know the best way to solve any problem.

Well, guess what my friend, You are wrong!

You don't have it all in you, you never did and you would probably never will. Because no man can master even one craft, let alone every. You need to do your homework for everything in your life, you try to master everything you come across but you can never really do so because you are a human. It is humanly impossible to be perfect at everything.

So stop calling yourself a saint or a self-taught genius because you are not.

You have this habit of lying to yourself because you find an escape from your faults. You find a way to cope with your inabilities. You find a way to soothe yourself that you are not wrong, just because everyone else says so.

You have to understand the fact that life has a way to be lived, and it is never the way of denial. It is rather the hopeful and quiet way of living your life with hard work and freedom.

You have to make your life worth living for. Because you know it in the back of your head that you have done the necessary hard work before to be able to compete among the best of the best out there.

You must have a strong feeling of justice towards yourself and towards others that makes you feel deserving of the highest honors and the biggest riches. Because you worked your whole life to be able to stand here and be a nominee for what life has to offer the best

Chapter 8:

Removing The Things In Your Day That Don't Serve A Purpose for You

Today I went to a yoga class and felt that something was not quite right. I did not enjoy it as much as I used to. As I was acting out the poses that the teacher was instructing to us, i found myself wondering what the heck I was doing on my yoga mat. Something i used to look forward everyday suddenly became a chore to me, and I didn't understand why.

I had been forcing myself for the past month thinking that I needed the class to stretch and to feel more flexible. But the more i attended, the unhappier I was. And it was only after I decided to completely remove yoga from my itinerary did I feel my day was actually more enjoyable.

Many times we plan things in our day just for the sake of it. We plan things because we think we have to, even if it didn't bring much joy into our lives.

I would like you to think of some of the things in your week, what are those that don't bring joy to you? Could you replace them with something that you might find a little more enjoyable instead?

i believe that many of us try to pack so much into our schedule thinking that the busier we are, the more meaningful our lives are, the more we are getting out of it. While it might be true to a certain extent, over doing and over subscribing can actually be counter-productive for us. All of us need rest and relaxation to recharge and tackle the next day. If we are packing our schedule of things we hate, we will never truly be at peace in life. It is okay to stop the things that stop bringing you joy, and maybe coming back to it at a later time.

I found myself loving to spend time stretching by myself while listening to music rather than doing it in a yoga class. And as soon as I replaced this block of time with something that I enjoyed, it made my day that much better, even if it was just a little.

Start taking a hard look at everything we are putting our time, energy, and commitment to, what are the areas that we should trim that don't serve us anymore, and how can we either replace them with something better or just freeing up time to rest and sleep instead until we figure it out.

You may find yourself just a little bit happier.

Chapter 9:

How to find inner peace and happiness – 10 things you can start doing today

Today's life is increasingly hectic and unorganized. We're running a race to accomplish more. And this race to nowhere has brought increased stress, anxiety, and even depression for some of us. In the process we have lost peace, harmony, and organization in our lives. That's the reason many among us have turned around in search of inner peace.

We must be mindful that inner peace is not something that we can just simply switch on when we decide we need it.

Inner peace is a state of mind that more often than not requires a lifelong journey of self-discovery and soul-searching. It is worthwhile to keep working towards finding and attaining that restful peace of mind, heart, and soul that we all deserve in our lives.

So the question here arises is, "What is inner peace, and how one can find it?"

Achieving Inner peace and happiness is possible, and you don't need to meditate on top of a mountain to break the barrier to find peace inside you.

If you want to achieve inner peace, here are 10 things you can start right now in your life.

1. Carve out some time for yourself

Take time out of your busy schedule and just be alone with yourself. Instead of constantly seeking happiness externally, look inwards to find serenity. Instead of trying to derive happiness from your friends or physical things, really discover how you can be happy without external influences. Can you be happy simply being alone with your thoughts and desires? Can you strive to achieve a calm state of mind that is free of worries and problems? Or is there something you know you need to do but have been putting off for quite some time? Only when you look inwards can you discover more about what truly matters to you.

2. Set Boundaries.

If you are feeling overwhelmed and exhausted, it is because you are doing things that are actually causing you to feel more anxious and stressed out. Consider setting boundaries to your bad habits, procrastinations, addictions, and even to technology such as your phone time and social media. It is truly time to stop doing the unnecessary things that don't move the needle forward for us and to start making time for important things in your life.Spending time with people who don't really care about your well-being or growth is something that we also need to be mindful of. Set a limit on the time we engage in those relationship and instead make more room for yourself to look inwards.

3. Find Your Relaxation Mojo

Everyone has their own unique relaxation mojo – For some it is to exercise, for some it is to read, and for others spending time family or listening to music helps calms them down. You know exactly what makes you tick. After you have identified what that is, simply make time to do more of it in the day or week. The goal is to release any tension you may have and to recharge your engines for what lies ahead.

4. Avoid turning molehills into mountains.

This is something that many of us might struggle with. We take a small problem and turn it into a giant mammoth task, causing us to lose our stability in the process while also creating unwanted stress in our lives. We will never find peace and happiness if we amplify every small little issue that may rise up. Instead work on breaking these things down even further to make them manageable and fun to do.

5. Keep an eye on your emotions

It is easy to let our emotions rule our actions. If we are not mindful of how we manage the stressors that life will throw at us from day to day, we may end up becoming bitter people by the end of it all. Always find a way to release these negative emotions in a way that works for you. Allow space for positive energy to fill up those spaces after you've successfully detoxed yourself. If something is simply too overwhelming and it is causing you to be angry, stressed, anxious, and even burnt out, consider take a break from it completely and coming back to it once you have a clearer head and mind.

6. Unclutter your world, unclutter your mind.

Clutter is what causes confusion and chaos in our lives. Physical clutter from overwhelming amounts of stuff in your room, home, and workspace will also cause mental clutter in your mind. A tidy, uncluttered, and neat space is to best way to bring clarity to your thoughts. Sometimes we let our mind be filled with junk as well. From unhealthy thought patterns to ruminations of the past, we need to purge these from our system in order to truly find peace and happiness. Take the time to sort these out in all areas if your life. Your body and mind will greatly appreciate the effort.

7. Adopt a Minimalistic approach

You don't need a castle to live in, 100 dishes on your dining table, and a gigantic office to work.

One can live in a small apartment with a few rooms, eat simple food, and just have a table and chair for work. All you really need is a comfortable space where you can work and live smartly. A minimalistic approach towards life will bring peace of mind, reduce stress, and make the journey of achieving inner peace much easier for you.

8. Accept and let go.

One of the biggest hindrances between you and your search for inner peace is your reluctance to let go. Bad things happen to the best of us. Setbacks are inevitable. Instead of dwelling on your failures, celebrate your achievements instead. You are not the sum of your failures. Your failures are what makes you a better person. Don't hold yourself hostage for these feelings. Accept that setbacks are part of the game and simply look forward to the wonderful things that lie ahead.

9. Stop guessing.

Guessing and second guessing ourselves and others will never bring inner peace and happiness for us – it only serves to bring about uncertainty and hesitation. Instead of flipping a coin on every situation or decision, really dig deeper to find out whether something is truly what you want or need. Communicate these thoughts and feelings openly and honestly, it can save you from disappointment and misguided realities in the future.

10. Find The True Cause of Your Anxieties

Sometimes we waste our energy solving the wrong problems, and we go round and round searching for the reasons for our unhappiness. Ask yourself the right questions and find out what is really causing you pain. You may have subconsciously decided to bury it by hiding it under the carpet. It is always easier for us to escape and bury our heads in the sand when things get hard, but the pain will come back to haunt us eventually. Dig out these problems and anxieties and face them head on.

Bonus

Remember: There's always tomorrow

Sometimes life puts you on a harder path and you feel that this is not what you signed up for. But remember that there is always another day, another tomorrow. There is a season for everything and your time in the sun will come. Accept things as the way they are. Be patient and I firmly believe that good things will come to you.

Chapter 10:

How To Succeed In Life

"You can't climb the ladder of success with your hands in your pocket."

Every day that you're living, make a habit of making the most out of it. Make a habit of winning today. Don't dwell on the past, don't worry about the future. You just have to make sure that you're winning today. Move a little forward every day; take a little step every day. And when you're giving your fruitful efforts, you're making sure you're achieving your day, then you start to built confidence within yourselves. Confidence is when you close your eyes at night and see a vision, a dream, a goal, and you believe that you're going to achieve it. When you're doing things, when you're productive the whole day, then that long journey will become short in a matter of time.

Make yourself a power list for each day. Take a sheet of paper, write Monday on top of it and then write five critical, productive, actionable tasks that you're going to do that day. After doing the task, cross it off. Repeat the process every day of every week of every month till you get closer to achieving your goals, your dreams. It doesn't matter if you're doing the same tasks every day or how minor or major they are; what matters is that it's creating momentum in things that you've believed you couldn't do. And as soon as the momentum gets completed, you start to believe that you can do something. You eventually stop writing your tasks down because now they've become your new habits. You need a reminder for them. You don't need to cross them off because you're going to do them. The power list helps you win the day. You're stepping out of your comfort zone, doing something that looks uncomfortable for starters, but while doing this, even for a year, you will see yourself standing five years from where you're standing today.

Decide, commit, act, succeed, repeat. If you want to be an inspiration to others, a motivator to others, impact others somehow, you have to self-evaluate certain perceptions and think that'll help you change the way you see yourself and the world. Perseverance, hard-working, and consistency would be the keywords if one were to achieve success in life. You just have to keep yourself focused on your ultimate goal. You will fall a hundred times. There's always stumbling on the way. But if you have the skill, the power, the instinct to get yourself back up every time you fall, and to dig yourself out of the whole, then no one can stop you. You have to control the situation, Don't ever let the situation control you. You're living life exactly as it should be. If you don't like what you're living in, then consider changing the aspects. The person you are right now versus the person you want to be in the future, there's only a fine line between the two that you have to come face-to-face with.

Your creativity is at most powerful the moment you open your eyes and start your day. That's when you get the opportunity to steer your emotions and thoughts in the direction that you want them to go, not the other way around. Every failure is a step closer to success. We won't succeed on the first try, and we will never have it perfect by trying it only once. But we can master the art of not giving up. We dare to take risks. If we never fail, we never get the chance of getting something we never had. We can never taste the fruits of success without falling. The difference between successful people and those who aren't successful is the point of giving up.

Success isn't about perfection. Instead, it's about getting out of bed each day, clearing the dust off you, and thinking like a champion, a winner, going on about your day, being productive, and making the most out of it. Remember that the mind controls your body; your body doesn't hold your mind. You have to make yourself mentally tough to overcome the fears and challenges that come in the way of your goals. As soon as you get up in the morning, start thinking about anything or anyone that you're grateful for. Your focus should be on making yourself feel good and confident enough to get yourself through the day.

The negative emotions that we experience, like pain or rejection, or frustration, cannot always make our lives miserable. Instead, we can consider them as our most incredible friends that'll drive us to success. When people succeed, they tend to party. When they fail, they tend to ponder. And the pondering helps us get the most victories in our lives. You're here, into another day, still breathing fine, that means you got another chance, to better yourself, to be able to right your wrongs. Everyone has a more significant potential than the roles they put themselves in.

Trust yourself always. Trust your instinct—no matter what or how anyone thinks. You're perfectly capable of doing things your way. Even if they go wrong, you always learn something from them. Don't ever listen to the naysayers. You've probably heard a million times that you can't do this and you can't do that, or it's never even been done before. So what? So what if no one has ever done it before. That's more of the reason for you to do it since you'll become the first person to do it. Change that 'You can't' into 'Yes, I definitely can.' Muhammad Ali, one of the greatest boxers to walk on the face of this planet, was once asked, 'how many sit-ups do you do?' to which he replied, 'I don't count my sit-ups. I only start counting when it starts hurting. When I feel pain, that's when I start counting because that's when it really counts.' So we get a wonderful lesson to work tirelessly and shamelessly if we were to achieve our dreams. Dr. Arnold Schwarzenegger beautifully summed up life's successes in 6 simple rules; Trust yourself, Break some rules, Don't be afraid to fail, Ignore the naysayers, Work like hell, And give something back.

PART 2

Chapter 1:

Happy People Take Care of Themselves

I frequently hear the word "selfish" tossed about in coaching, often with a negative connotation. Someone feels bad that they were selfish or that someone else was selfish, and it was offensive. Selfishness – the lack of considering others or only being concerned with your advantage – can be a great weakness. The ability to put others' needs in front of your own is an important life skill that you need to be able to do without resentment, even when it's completely inconvenient and a sacrifice.

However, I would argue that the motivation behind that decision should be self-serving. In most cases, being selfish is just a matter of perspective, critical to happiness and self-evolution.

Let me explain…

First, let's talk about why it is so important to be selfish. As author Brené Brown has discovered in her research on wholehearted living, loving yourself more than you love others is the first and most critical step to seeking happiness and fulfillment.

She says it is impossible to love anyone more than you love yourself. Taking care of yourself is the pathway to fulfillment and high performance in work and life. And, just as importantly, it's a gift to others.

When your needs are met, and you feel good about yourself, it's easier to elevate other people's needs in front of your own. It's easy to be a giver when your cup is full. When you feel half-full or empty, it's harder to give. You inherently feel people should be giving more to you or others, so you don't have to give so much or feel you need to preserve more for yourself.

Here are the two common derailments that can prevent you from finding fulfillment:

1. <u>Giving too much</u>

When people give too much - continually put other people's needs ahead of their own - builds resentment and takes away from their ability to take care of themselves. When their time is so focused on others, they don't have any time left for themselves. I find people do this when they are uncomfortable asking for their needs, speaking up about issues, or delegating responsibilities. Often they hide these weaknesses by focusing on other people, so they don't have to focus on themselves. This not only leads to feeling unfulfilled but becomes a burden on others who feel they need to take care of the "giver."

2. <u>Taking too much time for ourselves</u>

On the opposite end of the spectrum, some people take too much time for themselves, mistakenly thinking it will lead to fulfillment. They do not "give" enough, and it usually makes them feel worse, disengaging them from relationships and putting them on a treadmill of trying to do something that will finally make them feel good. In these cases, they are usually working on the wrong issues. The places where they are investing their time do not give them meaning.

Chapter 2:

Having a Balanced Life

Today we're going to talk about how and why you should strive to achieve a balanced life. A balance between work, play, family, friends, and just time alone to yourself.

We all tend to lead busy lives. At some points we shift our entire focus onto something at the expense of other areas that are equally important.

I remember the time when I just got a new office space. I was so excited to work that i spent almost 95% of the week at the office. I couldn't for the life of me figured why i was so addicted to going to the office that I failed to see I was neglecting my family, my friends, my relationships. Soon after the novelty effect wore off, i found myself burnt out, distant from my friends and family, and sadly also found myself in a strained relationship.

This distance was created by me and me alone. I had forgotten what my priorities were. I hadn't realized that I had thrown my life completely off balance. I found myself missing the time I spent with my family and friends. And I found myself having to repair a strained relationship due to my lack of care and concern for the other party.

What you think is right in the moment, to focus on something exclusively at the expense of all else, may seem enticing. It may seem like there is nothing wrong with it. But dig deeper and check to make sure it is truly worth the sacrifice you are willing to make in other areas of your life.

It is easy for us to fall into the trap of wanting to make more money, wanting to work harder, to be career driven and all that. But what is the point in having more money if you don't have anyone to spend in on or spend it with? What's the point in having a nice car or a nice designer handbag if you don't have anyone to show it to?

Creating balance in our lives is a choice. We have the choice to carve out time in our schedule for the things that truly matter. Only when we know how to prioritise our day, our week, our month, can we truly find consistency and stability in our lives.

I know some people might say disagree with what I am sharing with you all today, but this is coming from my personal life experience. It was only after realising that I had broken down all the things I had worked so hard to build prior to this new work venture, that I started to see the bigger picture again.

That I didn't want to go down this path and find myself 30 years later regretting that I had not spent time with my family before they passed away, that I was all alone in this world without someone I can lean my shoulder on to walk this journey with me, that I didn't have any friends that I could call up on a Tuesday afternoon to have lunch with me because everyone thought of me as a flaker who didn't prioritise them in the their lives before.

Choose the kind of life you want for yourself. If what I have to say resonates with you, start writing down the things that you know you have not been paying much attention to lately because of something else that you chose to do. Whether it be your lover, your friends, a hobby, a passion project, whatever it may be. Start doing it again. The time to create balance is now.

Chapter 3:
How To Improve Your
Communication Skills

Today we're going to talk about a topic that could help you be a better communicator with your spouse, your friends, and even your colleagues and bosses. Being able to express yourself fluently and eloquently is a skill that is incredibly important as it allows us to express our thoughts and ideas freely and fluently in ways that others might understand.

When we are able to communicate easily with others, we are able to build instant rapport with them and this allows us to appear better than we actually are. We may be able to cover some of our flaws if we are able to communicate our strengths better.

So how do we actually become better communicators? I believe that the easiest way to begin is to basically start talking with more people. It is my experience that after spending much time on my own without much social interaction, that i saw my standard of communication dropped quite drastically. You see, being able to talk well is essentially a social skill, and without regular practice and use, you just simply can't improve it. I saw that with irregular use of social interaction, the only skill that actually improved for me was texting. And we all know that texting is a very impersonal way to communicate and does not actually translate to real world fluency in person to person conversations.

Similarly, watching videos on communication and reading tips and tricks really does not help at all unless you apply it in the real world. And to have regular practice, you need to start by either inviting all your friends out to a meal so that you can strike up conversations and improve from there, or by maybe joining a social interaction group class of sorts that would allow you to practice verbal communication skills. If u were to ask me, I believe that making the effort to speak to your friends and colleagues is the best way to begin. And you can even ask them for feedback if there are any areas that they find you could improve on. Expect genuine feedback and criticisms as they go if you hope to improve, and do not take them personally.

It is with my personal experience that i became extremely rusty when it came to talking to friends at one point in my life, when i was sort of living in isolation. I find it hard to connect even with my best friend, and i found it hard to find topics to discuss about, mainly because i wasn't really living much to begin with, and there was nothing i was experiencing in life that was really worth sharing. If you stop living life, you stop having significant moments, you stop having problems that need solving, and you stop having friends that needs supporting. I believe the best way is to really try to engage the person you are talking to by asking them very thoughtful questions and by being genuinely interested in what they have to say. Which also coincidentally ties into my previous video about being a good listener. which you should definitely check out if you haven't done so already.

Being a good listener is also a big part of being a good communicator. The other part being able to respond in a very insightful way that isn't patronising. We can only truly connect with the person we are talking to if we are able to first understand on an empathetic level, what they are going through, and then to reply with the same level of compassion and empathy that they require of us.

With colleagues and bosses, we should be able to strike up conversations that are professional yet natural. And being natural in the way we communicate takes practice from all the other social interactions that precede us.

I believe that being a good communicator really takes time and regular practice in order for it to come one day and just click for us. For a start, just simply try to be friendly and place yourself out of your comfort zone, only then can you start to see improvements.

I challenge each and everyone of you today who are striving to be better communicators to start asking out your friends and colleagues for coffees and dinners. Get the ball rolling and just simply start talking. Over time, it will just come naturally to you. Trust me.

Chapter 4:

Happy People Reward Themselves

Do you ever wonder if the carrot and stick principle would still work in this world? The answer to this would be yes, the reward and punishment system still works, and you can always leverage it to build good habits. They, in turn, will help you reach your goal faster; that is why it is essential to celebrate your hard work and then afterward reward yourself for the effort you have been putting in. Gretchen Rubin, in her book Better than before, says,

"When we give ourselves treats, we feel energized, cared for, and contented, which boosts our self-command — and self-command helps us maintain our healthy habits."

If you do not get any rewards and treats, you will feel resentful angry, and you feel depleted. Imagine putting in all the hard work and then not getting anything in return. How would that make you feel? Bad, right? That is precisely why rewarding yourself is essential. We are going to outline 2 simple reasons why rewarding yourself is important.

1. Reward makes you feel good and drives you further.

How do you train pets, your dogs, and cats? You teach them with a treat. Just like them, our brain works the same way we can train ourselves to do a lot more work by rewarding ourselves. When you give yourself a treat, you will boost your mood, making you happy. When you give yourself a treat, your brain releases a chemical called dopamine that makes you feel good and happy. Even tho it is important to reward yourself, not all rewards give the same effect, and you should choose wisely so that those treats create positive reinforcement.

2. It works as positive reinforcement.

When a pleasant outcome follows your behavior, you are more likely to repeat the behavior. And this is called positive reinforcement. Connecting your hard work to rewards effectively not only gives you a mental break but also motivates you to want to do more of it. Therefore, use treats as positive reinforcement to build your momentum and grow your habits.

Just like this powerful saying from Tony Robbins:

"People who succeed have momentum. The more they succeed, the more they want to succeed, and the more they find a way to succeed. Similarly, when someone is failing, the tendency is to get on a downward spiral that can even become a self-fulfilling prophecy.

Chapter 5:

Happy People Find Reasons to Laugh and Forge Deep Connections

"...Making a connection with men and women through humour, happiness and laughter not only helps you make new friends, but it is the means to establish a strong, meaningful connection to people."

People always try to have a personality that attracts people and makes them feel comfortable around them. Utilizing their humour has been one of those ways to create new friendships. But once you start doing this, you will realize that this humorous nature has emotions and attitudes that comprise happiness and positivity. This will also help you create deep and meaningful connections that will last a lifetime.

When you intend to focus on humour to find deep connections, your subconscious mind starts focusing on positivity. You will slowly turn out to be more positive in your reasoning and conduct because awareness of what's funny is truly only demonstrative of one's very own bliss. In this manner, you're sustaining a more appealing, and that's just the beginning "contagious" attitude. Similarly, as we search out bliss in our everyday lives through satisfying work, leisure activities, individual interests and day to day life, so too do people seek out and wish to be encircled by joy on a relational level: joy and bitterness are contagious, and we as a whole wish to get the happy bug.

Humour helps fashion friendships since we wish to encircle ourselves with individuals who are glad. This way, our objective shouldn't just be to utilize humour to make new companions, however to zero in on the entirety of the uplifting perspectives and feelings that include an entertaining and carefree nature. By embodying satisfaction, inspiration, happiness, receptiveness and tranquillity, we sustain a more grounded and "contagious" state of being.

Historically there was a negative connotation attached to humour, but over the years, research was done, and it proved otherwise. In any case, research on humour has come into the daylight, with humour currently seen as a character strength. Good brain science, a field that analyzes what individuals progress admirably, notes that humour can be utilized to cause others to feel better, acquire closeness, or help buffer pressure. Alongside appreciation, expectation and otherworldliness, a funny bone has a place with the arrangement of qualities positive clinicians call greatness; together, they help us manufacture associations with the world and give significance to life. Enthusiasm for humour corresponds with different qualities, as well, like insight and love of learning. Furthermore, humour exercises or activities bring about expanded sensations of passionate prosperity and idealism.

Once you step into adulthood, it can be difficult for many people to form friendships and then keep up with them because all of us get busier in our lives. Still, it's never too much to go to a bar and strike up a conversation with a random person and believe us, if you have a good sense of humour, they will be naturally attracted towards you.

Chapter 6:

Happy People Dream Big

Remember being a kid, and when somebody asked you what you wanted to be after growing up, you answered with a big dream: an astronaut, a ballerina, a scientist, a firefighter, or the President of the United States. You believed that you could achieve anything you set your mind at that no dream is too big that if you wanted, you would make it happen. But why is it that so many adults forget what it is like to dream big. Happy people are dreamers; if you want to become a happy person, you need to make dreaming big a habit; some people even say that if your dreams do not scare you, you are not dreaming big. Now you must be wondering how dreaming big can make you happy. Firstly, it helps you see that if you had a magic wand and you could get whatever you wanted, what you would want for yourself, and there is a chance that these dreams are things you want to achieve in your life somehow other. Secondly, it will help you in removing any fears you have about not being able to achieve your dreams because when you dream big, you think about what you want in your ideal world, and your fear will not come in your way because you would feel like you are living in that fantasy world. Lastly, you will put your dreams and desires into the universe, and the likelihood of making those dreams come true increases. Fulfilling your dreams makes you happy because you will be able to get what you have yearned for so long, and a sense of achievement will make you feel confident about yourself and the dream you had. Now you must have a question what should I do to start dreaming big I am going to outline some of the things you can practice!

Sit back, clear your mind and think about your desires and dreams. What do you want in life? If you had three wishes from a genie, what are the things you would ask for? What is something you would if no one was looking or if you weren't afraid. Now write these dreams down on a piece of paper. This way, they would seem more real. The next thing you should do is start reading some inspirational books that motivate you to start living your best life starting today! Lastly, make a list of goals you want to achieve and start working on them.

Chapter 7:

Happy People Don't Sweat the Small Stuff.

Stress follows a peculiar principle: when life hits us with big crises—the death of a loved one or a job loss—we somehow find the inner strength to endure these upheavals in due course. It's the little things that drive us insane day after day—traffic congestion, awful service at a restaurant, an overbearing coworker taking credit for your work, meddling in-laws, for example.

It's all too easy to get caught up in the many irritations of life. We overdramatize and overreact to life's myriad tribulations. Under the direct influence of anguish, our minds are bewildered, and we feel disoriented. This creates stress, which makes the problems more difficult to deal with.

The central thesis of psychotherapist Richard Carlson's bestselling ***Doesn't Sweat The Small Stuff... And It's All Small Stuff*** (1997) is this: to deal with angst or anger, we need not some upbeat self-help prescriptions for changing ourselves, but simply a measure of perspective.

Perspective helps us understand that there's an art to understand what we should let go of and what we should concern ourselves with. It is important to focus our efforts on the important stuff and not waste time on insignificant and incidental things.

I've previously written about my favorite 5-5-5 technique for gaining perspective and guarding myself against anger erupting: I remove myself from the offending environment and contemplate if whatever I'm getting worked up over is of importance. I ask myself, "Will this matter in 5 days? Will this matter in 5 months? Will this matter in 5 years?"

Carlson stresses that there's always a vantage point from which even the biggest stressor can be effectively dealt with. The challenge is to keep making that shift in perspective. When we achieve that "wise-person-in-me" perspective, our problems seem more controllable and our lives more peaceful.

Carlson's prescriptions aren't uncommon—we can learn to be more patient, compassionate, generous, grateful, and kind, all of which will improve the way we feel about ourselves and how other people feel when they are around us.

Some of Carlson's 100 recommendations are trite and banal—for example, "make peace with imperfection," "think of your problems as potential teachers," "remember that when you die, your 'in-basket' won't be empty," and "do one thing at a time." Others are more informative:

- Let others have the glory
- Let others be "right" most of the time
- Become aware of your moods, and don't allow yourself to be fooled by the low ones
- Look beyond behavior
- Every day, tell at least one person something you like, admire, or appreciate about them.
- Argue for your limitations, and they're yours
- Resist the urge to criticize
- Read articles and books with entirely different points of view from your own and try to learn something.

Chapter 8:

Everything is A Marathon Not A Sprint

Ask your parents, what was it like to raise children till the time they were able to lift their weight and be self-sufficient. I am sure they will say, it was the most beautiful experience in their lives. But believe me, They are lying.

There is no doubt in it that what you are today is because of your parents, and your parents didn't rest on their backs while a nanny was taking care of you.

They spent countless nights of sleeplessness changing diapers and soothing you so that you can have a good night's sleep. They did that because they wanted to see a part of them grow one day and become what they couldn't be. What you are today is because of their continuous struggle over the years.

You didn't grow up overnight, and your parents didn't teach you everything overnight. It took years for them to teach you and it took even more time for you to learn.

This is life!

Life is an amalgamation of little moments and each moment is more important than the last one.

Start with a small change. Learn new skills. The world around you changes every day. Don't get stuck in your routine life. Expand your horizons. What's making you money today might not even exist tomorrow. So why stick to it for the rest of your life.

You are never too old to learn new things. The day you stop learning is the last day of your life. A human being is the most supreme being in this universe for a reason. That reason is the intellect and the ability to keep moving with their lives.

You can never be a millionaire in one night. It's a one-in-billion chance to win a lottery and do that overnight. Most people see the results of their efforts in their next generation, but the efforts do pay off.

If you want to have eternal success. It will take an eternity of effort and struggles to get there. Because life is a marathon and a marathon tests your last breaths. But when it pays off, it is the highest you can get.

Shaping up a rock doesn't take one single hit, but hundreds of precision cuts with keen observation and attention. Life is that same rock, only bigger and much more difficult.

Changing your life won't happen overnight. Changing the way you see things won't happen overnight. It will take time.

To know everything and to pretend to know everything is the wrong approach to life. It's about progress. It's about learning a little bit at each step along the way.

To evolve, to adapt, to figure out things as they come, is the process of life that every living being in this universe has gone through before and will continue to go through in the future. We are who we are because of the marathon of life.

Every one of us today has more powerful things in our possessions right now than our previous 4 generations combined. So we are lucky to be in this world, in this era.

We have unlimited resources at our disposal, but we still can't get things in the blink of an eye. Because no matter how evolved we are, we still are a slave to the reality of nature, and that reality is the time itself!

If you are taking each step to expect a treat at each stop, you might not get anything. But if you believe that each step that you take is a piece in a puzzle, a puzzle that becomes a picture that is far beautiful and meaningful, believe me, the sky is your limit.

Life is a set of goals. You push and grind to get these goals but when you get there you realize that there is so much more to go on and achieve.

Committing to a goal is difficult but watching your dreams come true is something worth fighting for.

You might not see it today, you might not see it 2 years from now, but the finish line is always one step closer. Life has always been and always will be a race to the top. But only the ones who make it to the top have gone through a series of marathons and felt the grind throughout everything.

Your best is yet to come but is on the other end of that finish line.

Chapter 9:

10 Habits For A Clean Home

A clean home can make the homeowner a lot happier, less stressed, and even calmer. Waking up or coming back to a clutter-free and organized home can instantly brighten our mornings or even lift up our moods. But the thought of having to clean it extensively on weekends, for long hours, only to find the space in an absolute mess by midweek is like a nightmare and crestfallen.

Trust me when I say it is not that difficult maintaining a clean home. You need not necessarily have to deep clean your house almost every weekend for hours if you incorporate few very habits in your everyday routines. Today, we are exactly going to talk on this topic and hope to enlighten you to create a clean space.

Here are ten habits for a clean and happy home:

1. Make Your Bed As Soon as You Wake Up

We have heard a million times that the first thing that we should do after waking up is to make our beds, but how many of us incorporate this habit daily? An unmade bed can pull down the overall appearance of your bedroom by making it look messy. So take few moments and tuck those sheets and put your pillows in order. Change your bed sheets or duvet covers, and pillow covers as and when necessary.

Making our beds clean our most comfortable and visible area in the house and gives a sense of achievement helps us stay motivated and in a fresh state of mind throughout the day. If tucking in bed sheets daily is too annoying for you simply switch to duvet covers; that might save you from some hassle.

2. Put Things Back in Place After Using Them

Almost every home has this one chair or one spot that is cluttered with clothes and random knick-knacks, and this area hardly gets cleaned. Moreover, it is a normal human tendency to go on to dump more and more pieces of stuff and increase the pile size.

The idea behind creating this pile is that you will put away all the things in one go in a single day, but who are we kidding? As the pile starts increasing, we start pushing away the task of keeping the things back in their original place. The best way to avoid creating clutter is to put things back in their true place as soon as their job is done.

I completely understand that after finishing a task, we never feel like getting up to put them back in their home and hinder the task until we feel like doing so. But if you can consciously put this little effort into not letting things sit on the ground or in random places and put them back as soon as their job is done for the day, it is going to save a lot of time and help you have a clean space.

This is also applicable to your freshly washed clothes. As soon as you have them cleaned, fold them and put them in the drawer where it belongs. This will save you the headache of doing so on a Saturday morning which can then be used for reading your favorite book.

3. Take Your Mess With You as You Leave the Room

This is another essential practice that can bring a huge difference in your life and your home if turned into a habit. The idea here is to try not to leave a room empty-handed. What does this mean?

Let us take an example to understand this. Suppose you are in your living room and are going to the kitchen to drink water. Before you leave the living room, scan the room and look if any dirty bowl or plate is sitting in the room that needs to go to the kitchen. Take that cutlery along with you and keep them in the sink or dishwasher.

After making this a habit, you can then start following the one-touch rule that states that you touch a used item only once! That means if you are taking out the trash, make sure to dump or dispose of it properly and not just take it out and keep it somewhere on the porch or garden as this will kill the whole idea behind the habit. If you are moving something, it is better that you keep them where they belong, else, leave them be.

4. Have a House Cleaning Schedule

Maintain cleaning schedules like morning cleaning routines or weekly cleaning routines. This is basically distributing the cleaning of the entire house over an entire week rather than keeping the task to get done in a single day. Fix days for achieving a particular task, like on Wednesdays you can vacuum the living room and the bedroom and on Thursdays clean the other rooms and so on.

Make sure to assign 15 to 20 minutes each morning that you will strictly use for cleaning purposes. This will surely bring about a very positive impact on your house, and you will be in awe of how much cleaning can be done in those mere 15 - 20 minutes. Try to vacuum the hallways, entries, and all other high traffic regions of your home (including the kitchen) as frequently as possible as they tend to get dusty easily.

5. Maintain a Laundry Routine

Maintain a proper laundry routine depending on whether you live alone or in a family. As the pile of clothes grows enough to go into the washing, do the needful immediately. Do not delay the task endlessly as remember it is always easier to wash one load of clothing at a day rather than washing multiple loads of cloth in a day.

If you live with a family, do laundry every alternate day and if you live alone, then make sure to do your laundry every weekend. Also, make it a habit of putting the dirty clothes in the basket immediately after changing out of it rather than keeping them at random places to wash them later.

6. Keep Your Shoes, Coats, and Umbrellas in Their Right Place

Make it a habit to open your shoes near the entrance, put them away properly, and not randomly throw them. Keep a basket near the entryway where you can store all the umbrellas. If possible, put up a key holder on the door to keep the car keys and door keys in an organized manner.

The same goes for your long coats. Do not just dump them anywhere right after returning home! Have hooks hidden behind the entry door or have a sleek cupboard near the exit to store the trenchcoats and the long coats away from sight. These little changes will instantly clean up space.

7. Relax Only After Finishing Your Chores

If you have a chore that requires immediate attention, do it! Do not sit and relax, as this will go on to delay the chore indefinitely, and you may even forget to do it. So get your chores done first, then sit and watch Netflix. Detain your tasks only when you are exhausted and desperately need a break.

8. Clean After Every Meal

Right after fishing your meal, clean up the place. I know what most of you are thinking, but trust me, relaxing after cleaning everything up will give you more satisfaction and help you have a cleaner home for sure. After having your lunch or dinner, keep all the plates in the washer and make sure to also clean the utensils that you used for cooking.

Clean the countertops, the burners, and also the table that you sat and ate on. Cleaning the countertops and tables immediately will save your furniture from an ugly stain and help you save a lot of energy and time you might have had to put in if you try to clean the spill the later day.

9. Clean Your Dishes and Sink Every Night

I wanted to say have a nighttime cleaning routine every day where you clean all the dishes from dinner or any other remaining dishes of the day, the sink, and the kitchen by placing all the ingredient containers in their rightful places. The nighttime routine would also include setting your dining table, setting the cushions on your sofa, and clearing out your fridge so that you have a clean and spacious fridge before you unpack your groceries.

But I understand that not many of us have the energy after a hectic day at work, so instead of doing the entire routine, just make sure to wash all the dishes and clean the sink thoroughly so that you wake up to a beautiful kitchen in the morning. I mean, who wants to wake up to a pile of dishes, right? Just give some extra time at night to clean out the kitchen to have a fresh start in the morning.

10. Get Rid Of Unnecessary Things

To have a clutter-free space, each item in your home must have a home of its own. For example, if you do not have a place to hang your towels, they will likely be lying here and there and making the space look messy. Thus, make sure each item has its own place to sleep. If you see there are free-flowing items, then it is time to declutter!

You do not need much space, but you definitely need fewer items that fit in the available space and are easier to manage. More items require more time to clean and put things away properly. Thus, it is easier and requires less time to clean a room with lesser items out on the floor or on the countertop. Hence, make it a habit of getting rid of all the unnecessary items. You can donate the items or gift them to your neighbors or friends. Recycle all the old newspaper and magazines as papers too contribute a lot to the messiness of any room.

Extra Tip: Always try to keep your cleaning supplies in easily visible and accessible areas. This will save you a lot of time and motivate you to clean up anything that should be done as soon as possible.

Be satisfied with clean enough! A home can neither be squeaky clean every day nor can it be cleaned in one day. It is a gradual process that requires a conscious effort being made daily.

A clean home can be easily achieved by following these tips and manifesting these practices as your daily habits.

Chapter 10:

9 Signs You're Feeling Insecure About a Relationship

Being in a new relationship is often the most exciting part. You go back and forth with your date, wondering if he or she likes you, and you play the dating game as all new romance starts out. But what happens when you start to fall for someone more than you thought you would have liked to at this stage.

It is never a pleasant feeling for us to feel that we are not in control, but that is the process of being vulnerable and admitting to yourself that you do have a personal investment in this relationship. If you are unsure about what you are going through,

Here are 7 Signs That Show You Are Feeling Insecure About A Relationship:

1. You Start Checking Their "Last Seen"

We have all done this before - We wonder why it takes so long for the person to reply our texts so we check our messaging apps constantly to check when they were last online. We then draw deductions that they may have deliberately chosen not to reply to our messages despite being online. However unhealthy habit of checking their "last seen" only takes power away from our self-worth. We need to stop obsessing over such small little details and just focus on the things we are supposed to do for the day. If the person genuinely likes you, he or she will find the time to reply in a thoughtful and appropriate manner.

2. You Anxiously Hope That They Ask You Out

Waiting for the next date to happen is normal. We all expect to have some back and forth to ensure that it is not a one-sided effort in dating and relationships. However, if this becomes an anxious wait, then you might be falling into the realm of insecurity. Ideally things should happen naturally if all is going well. If you catch yourself losing sleep because he or she hasn't asked you out, take some of that power back and consider taking the initiative instead to either ask if there is going to be a next date, or even asking them out if you want to see this through. Don't let anxiety rule your dating life.

3.   You Wait For Them To Say Something Sweet To Affirm Their Like of you

We all want to be woo-ed. It is a nice feeling when someone says something sweet to you just because. But if you find yourself eagerly anticipating every sentence to be something affectionate, be careful not to be disappointed if it doesn't happen ever-so-often. Dating and relationships can be a tricky business; we don't want to seem too needy or too forward at the same time. Sometimes we just have to find a balance between being overly sweet and also reserving some of it when so as not to come across too strong.

4.   You Start Thinking Of The Worst-Case Scenarios

Being in the early phases of a relationship is always fun, but as the dust settles and you start thinking of the worst-case scenarios, you may be feeling insecure. We all want to go back to the part of dating where we expect nothing from the other party - we are dating a few different people at once and we have no desires to commit. But when you start catching yourself thinking of what could go wrong with someone you've decided you like more than others, it may be time to take a step back and reassess the situation. Don't jump too far ahead of the curve.

5.   You Can't Focus On Your Work

Being in love and thinking about the wonderful things about the other person is a normal way to lose focus on your work. However if this lack of concentration starts revolving around worry that things could go wrong, or that the person may not like you, then you've got to snap out of it. It is never healthy to let these negative thoughts affect your daily productivity. Remember that your life always comes first - Focus on the important things and then worry about dating and relationships later.

6.   You're Distraught From The Lack of Clear Signals

You find yourself second guessing everything. One minute you think your date is interested, the next you're worried he or she is not. This back and forth can take a toll on your mental capacity to handle things and you may find yourself feeling out of sorts. You wonder if your date went well or did it go disastrously. The fact that your date isn't giving you any clear signs adds to your insecurity about the whole thing.

7.   You're Unsure About Where This Is Going

Similar to the previous point, this time you are unsure where this relationship is headed. Is there something there or should you cut your losses and move on. It will be hard to assess the situation and the only way to be sure is to ask him or her directly what their thoughts are about the whole matter. If they are unable to give you a clear answer, you can at least be assured that it is not all in your head. Do what is best for yourself and never be too hung up over just one person.

8.   You Wonder If They Are Seeing Someone Else

This is insecurity at one of the highest levels. Trust is something that must be built over time. If you find yourself questioning whether your date or partner is seeing someone else, maybe you never really felt secure in this relationship in the first place. This could be a tricky matter to handle so once again if you find yourself doubting every aspect of this bond, maybe it's time to be dial it back until you can trust your whole heart with that person.

9.   You Question Every Single Decision You Make

Second guessing ourselves and everything that we do has got to be one of the worst ways to operate in life. You question whether you said the right thing on the date, whether you made the right moves, whether you came off as confident rather weak. These are questions that we need to not bother ourselves with because it will not bring any goodness to us. Make decisions that you will stick with no matter what and stop ruminating on the past. Just do what you can now and move forward with pride.

Conclusion

Dating and relationships are not easy. It comes with its own set of rules and emotions are bound to run rampant at some point if we don't reign them in. Instead of making it harder than it already is for ourselves, simply trust that things will work out if it's meant to be. Overthinking and feeling insecure will not bring us any good. The fact is that sometimes we will get our hearts broken, but we will stand tall and learn from our past. The quest for love is not going to be a piece of cake, but if the right person comes along, things will work out.

PART 3

Chapter 1:

8 Ways To Love Yourself First

"Your task is not to seek for love, but merely to seek and find all the barriers within yourself that you have built against it." - Rumi.

Most of us are so busy waiting for someone to come into our lives and love us that we have forgotten about the one person we need to love the most – ourselves. Most psychologists agree that being loved and being able to love is crucial to our happiness. As quoted by Sigmund Freud, "love and work ... work and love. That's all there is." It is the mere relationship of us with ourselves that sets the foundation for all other relationships and reveals if we will have a healthy relationship or a toxic one.

Here are some tips on loving yourself first before searching for any kind of love in your life.

1. Know That Self-Love Is Beautiful

Don't ever consider self-love as being narcissistic or selfish, and these are two completely different things. Self-love is rather having positive regard for our wellbeing and happiness. When we adopt self-love, we see higher levels of self-esteem within ourselves, are less critical and harsh with ourselves while making mistakes, and can celebrate our positive qualities and accept all our negative ones.

2. Always be kind to yourself:

We are humans, and humans are tended to get subjected to hurts, shortcomings, and emotional pain. Even if our family, friends, or even our partners may berate us about our inadequacies, we must learn to accept ourselves with all our imperfections and flaws. We look for acceptance from others and be harsh on ourselves if they tend to be cruel or heartless with us. We should always focus on our many positive qualities, strengths, and abilities, and admirable traits; rather than harsh judgments, comparisons, and self-hatred get to us. Always be gentle with yourself.

3. Be the love you feel within yourself:

You may experience both self-love and self-hatred over time. But it would be best if you always tried to focus on self-love more. Try loving yourself and having positive affirmations. Do a love-kindness meditation or spiritual practices to nourish your soul, and it will help you feel love and compassion toward yourself. Try to be in that place of love throughout your day and infuse this love with whatever interaction you have with others.

4. Give yourself a break:

We don't constantly live in a good phase. No one is perfect, including ourselves. It's okay to not be at the top of your game every day, or be happy all the time, or love yourself always, or live without pain. Excuse your bad days and embrace all your imperfections and mistakes. Accept your negative emotions but don't let them overwhelm you. Don't set high standards for yourself, both emotionally and mentally. Don't judge yourself for whatever you feel, and always embrace your emotions wholeheartedly.

5. Embrace yourself:

Are you content to sit all alone because the feelings of anxiety, fear, guilt, or judgment will overwhelm you? Then you have to practice being comfortable in your skin. Go within and seek solace in yourself, practice moments of alone time and observe how you treat yourself. Allow yourself to be mindful of your beliefs, feelings, and thoughts, and embrace solitude. The process of loving yourself starts with understanding your true nature.

6. Be grateful:

Rhonda Bryne, the author of The Magic, advises, "When you are grateful for the things you have, no matter how small they may be, you will see those things instantly increase." Look around you and see all the things that you are blessed to have. Practice gratitude daily and be thankful for all the things, no matter how good or bad they are. You will immediately start loving yourself once you realize how much you have to be grateful for.

7. Be helpful to those around you:

You open the door for divine love the moment you decide to be kind and compassionate toward others. "I slept and dreamt that life was a joy. I awoke and saw that life was service. I acted, and behold, and service was a joy." - Rabindranath Tagore. The love and positive vibes that you wish upon others and send out to others will always find a way back to you. Your soul tends to rejoice when you are kind, considerate, and compassionate. You have achieved the highest form of self-love when you decide to serve others. By helping others, you will realize that you don't need someone else to feel complete; you are complete. It will help you feel more love and fulfillment in your life.

8. Do things you enjoy doing:

If you find yourself stuck in a monotonous loop, try to get some time out for yourself and do the things that you love. There must be a lot of hobbies and passions that you might have put a brake on. Dust them off and start doing them again. Whether it's playing any sport, learning a new skill, reading a new book, writing in on your journal, or simply cooking or baking for yourself, start doing it again. We shouldn't compromise on the things that make us feel alive. Doing the things we enjoy always makes us feel better about ourselves and boost our confidence.

Conclusion:

Loving yourself is nothing short of a challenge. It is crucial for your emotional health and ability to reach your best potential. But the good news is, we all have it within us to believe in ourselves and live the best life we possibly can. Find what you are passionate about, appreciate yourself, and be grateful for what's in your life. Accept yourself as it is.

Chapter 2:

8 Tips to Become More Resilient

Resilience shows how well you can deal with the problems life throws at you and how you bounce back. It also means whether you maintain a positive outlook and cope with stress effectively or lose your cool. Although some people are naturally resilient, research shows that these behaviors can be learned. So, whether you are going through a tough time right now or you want to be prepared for the next step in your life, here are eight techniques you can focus on to become more resilient.

1. Find a Sense of Purpose

When you are going through a crisis or a tragedy, you must find a sense of purpose for yourself; this can play an important role in your recovery. This can mean getting involved in your community and participating in activities that are meaningful to you so every day you would have something to look forward to, and your mind wouldn't be focusing on the tragedy solely. You will be able to get through the day.

2. Believe in Your Abilities

When you have confidence in yourself that you can cope with the issues in your life, it will play an important role in resilience; once you become confident in your abilities, it will be easier for you to respond and deal with a crisis. Listen to the negative comments in your head, and once you do, you need to practice replacing them with positive comments like I'm good at my job, I can do this, I am a great friend/partner/parent.

3.   Develop a Strong Social Network

It is very important to be surrounded by people you can talk to and confide in. When you have caring and supportive people around you during a crisis, they act as your protectors and make that time easier for you. When you are simply talking about your problems with a friend or a family member, it will, of course, not make your problem go away. Still, it allows you to share your feelings and get supportive feedback, and you might even be able to come up with possible solutions to your problems.

4.   Embrace Change

An essential part of resilience is flexibility, and you can achieve that by learning how to be more adaptable. You'll be better equipped to respond to a life crisis when you know this. When a person is resilient, they use such events as opportunities to branch out in new directions. However, it is very likely for some individuals to get crushed by abrupt changes, but when it comes to resilient individuals, they adapt to changes and thrive.

5.   Be Optimistic

It is difficult to stay optimistic when you are going through a dark period in your life, but an important part of resilience can maintain a hopeful outlook. What you are dealing with can be extremely difficult, but what will help you is maintaining a positive outlook about a brighter future. Now, positive thinking certainly does not mean that you ignore your problem to focus on the positive outcomes. This simply means understanding that setbacks don't always stay there and that you certainly have the skills and abilities to fight the challenges thrown at you.

6. Nurture Yourself

When you are under stress, it is easy not to take care of your needs. You can lose your appetite, ignore exercise, not get enough sleep. These are all very common reactions when you are stressed or are in a situation of crisis. That is why it is important to invest time in yourself, build yourself, and make time for activities you enjoy.

7. Develop Problem-Solving Skills

Research shows that when people are able to come up with solutions to a problem, it is easier for them to cope with problems compared to those who can not. So, whenever you encounter a new challenge, try making a list of potential ways you will be able to solve that problem. You can experiment with different strategies and eventually focus on developing a logical way to work through those problems. By practicing your problem-solving skills on a regular basis, you will be better prepared to cope when a serious challenge emerges.

8. Establish Goals

Crisis situations can be daunting, and they also seem insurmountable but resilient people can view these situations in a realistic way and set reasonable goals to deal with problems. So, when you are overwhelmed by a situation, take a step back and simply assess what is before you and then brainstorm possible solutions to that problem and then break them down into manageable steps.

Chapter 3:

Don't Set The Wrong Goals

Most people even though they are the most ambitious ones in their circle do not ever succeed. It's not because they are not capable. It's not because they don't have the effort and hard work for what it takes to be successful. It's certainly not because they haven't had the opportunity.

These people have a pattern for them. These people have all the right energies and all the right tools, but only the wrong motives. These people don't have the right goals.

When you set a goal, many things make you think of them. Most of the time there is an external motivation driving our goals. But why do we need someone else to realize a certain goal?

Yes, this is the biggest reason to set the wrong goals. You don't need some sense of insecurity or jealousy to be motivated and do something that you were never meant to do or become someone who you were never meant to be.

People often portray these feelings as an effort to be extra ambitious towards some pointless thing.

The majority of us don't know what we want in our lives. It is impossible to search for something meaningful when you don't have the faintest idea of anything even closer to what you want.

There are many other things wrong with our approach to setting goals. Most of us procrastinate. We exaggerate things beyond the point of achieving. What we don't realize is that when we are not able to achieve those unrealistic things, we get demotivated and start building fears and doubts. These are the biggest enemies of any success story.

Setting up goals is a process and we need to go through the process. The first step in this process is not to take anything for granted. Because isn't a single worthless thing in life.

Don't underestimate the time and don't rush. Everything happens in a due course and you cannot rush things and expect them to be perfect.

Similarly, you cannot expect to have success without going through a single failure. Failures have a big impact on our personal development. Because failures make us tough and experienced hard-working people that everyone wishes to be. So appreciate every failure and take it as a learning curve to carve out new goals with a different approach.

The final and the most essential step towards an achievable goal is to avoid setting up negative goals. If you want something, don't take the 'The Glass is half empty' approach. If you want to look good, don't aim that you want to lose fat, just imagine and aim that you want to get healthy.

Negative goals don't mean evil thoughts, but they are the wrong approach towards the right things and this is what forces us to make undesirable and emotionally hurtful goals that don't push you to be good. They rather make you stay demotivated and alone.

The last but not the least thing is to never get hasty and put too much in your basket. Take only what you can use at a certain time and by this rule, you must follow one goal at a time.

Chapter 4:

5 Ways To Deal with Personal Feelings of Inferiority

Have you at some point felt that you are inferior to others? That's normal. All of us, at some point in our lives, have felt the same. Growing up, we saw other kids who performed better than us in the class. Kids who played sports well. Kids who were loved by all. We got jealous. We felt inferior to them. We constantly compared ourselves to them.

Almost everyone has experienced that in their childhood. But do you still feel the same about others? Do you constantly analyze situations and people around you? Do you feel worthless? Then you probably have an inferiority complex. But the good news is you can get over this inferiority complex. We are going to list some of the things that will help you in doing that.

1. Build self-confidence

Treat yourself better. Act confident. Do what you love. Embrace yourself. Is there anything in your body that you don't feel confident about? Maybe your smile, your nose, or your hair? The trick here is to either accept yourself the way you are or do something about it. If you have curly hair, get your hair straightener. Do whatever makes you feel better about yourself.

2. Surround yourself with people who uplift you

It's important to realize that your inferiority complex might be linked to the people around you. It might be your relatives, your friends at college, your siblings, or your colleagues. Analyze your interactions with them.

Once you can identify people who try to pull you down, do not reciprocate your feelings, or are not very encouraging, start distancing yourself from them. Look for positive people, who uplift you, and who bring out the better version of yourself. Take efforts to develop a relationship with them.

3. Stop worrying about what other people think.

One major cause of inferiority complexes is constantly thinking about what others are thinking about us. We seek validation from them for every action of ours. Sometimes we are thinking about their actions, while sometimes, we imagine what they think.

4. Stop worrying about what other people think.

One major cause of inferiority complexes is constantly thinking about what others are thinking about us. We seek validation from them for every action of ours. Sometimes we are thinking about their actions, while sometimes, we are imagining what they think.

Disassociate yourself from their judgments. It's ultimately your opinion about yourself that matters. When we feel good about ourselves, others feel good about ourselves.

5. Do not be harsh on yourself.

There is no need to be harsh on yourself. Practice self-care. Love yourself. Be kind to yourself. Do not over-analyze situations. Do not expect yourself to change overnight. Give yourself time to heal.

Chapter 5:

8 Habits You Should Have For Life

The key to being happy, feeling energized, and having a productive life relies on a cycle of good habits. Achieving a state of spiritual and physical satisfaction is a conscious choice that you can make for yourself. Realize what attaining the greatest happiness means for you and strive to be as productive as you can to achieve that happiness. Work towards a sense of self-realization and start reaching for your goals one step at a time. Accomplishing this requires you to be confident and have a sense of self, built entirely on good habits. This includes having good attitudes, thoughts, and decision-making skills. Quoting the all-time favorite Poet- Maya Angelou, "a good life is achieved by liking who you are, what you do, and how you do it."

How do you put this in place? Living by good habits and discipline nourishes your potential and make you a better person in your surroundings.

Here are 8 habits you should adopt for life:

1. Create a clear Morning Routine That Is Non-Negotiable.

Creating a morning routine that you like and living up to it is essential. Before you start your day, you can turn to what you like doing be it running, meditating, or having a peaceful meal-time at breakfast. Whatever activities you choose based on your liking, kick start your day with that habit. Managing your morning routine and making it a habit enables you to start your day on a proactive and positive note. This will also help you in enhancing your mental health and productivity. Through trial and error find out what works best for you and stick to you day in and out.

2. Make a Point of Physically Exercising Your Body Muscles.

To jog your cognitive skills, relieve stress that has a hold on your performance stamina means that you need to exercise-go to the gym regularly or as much as you can. Do you still need more convincing reasons for hitting the gym? Here you go! Physical exercises increase your 'happy' moods chemically and propels the release of hormone endorphins. This hormone aids in getting rid of all the body and mind anxious feelings, hence enabling you to calm down.

3. Develop Quality Personal Relationships With Loved Ones.

The Harvard study of adult development has found that most of the existing long-term happiness for an individual is predicted through healthy relationships. Developing and maintaining close relationships with your loved ones or those close to people you consider family has been found to help someone live a longer and quality life. Hence it is the connections within your surroundings that make your life worthwhile.

4. Master an Attitude of Listening.

If you want to cultivate relationships in your life, be it professional or personal, communication is key. While communicating with your peers, family, or colleagues, you need to understand that listening to what they are saying is important. This is because you cannot have effective communication if it's one-sided. Remember that it is always important to value what others have to say. Their perspective might impact you, but most importantly, when you listen, you make others feel valued. Always try to understand the other party's point of view even if it defers from yours. Be open-minded to differing opinions. The more you listen, the more you get to learn.

➤ 5. Choose Natural Food Rather Than Processed Ones To Help Keep Your Brain Intact.

Whatever we eat always impacts our health, energy, moods, and concentration level. Whether you have weight issues or not, eating a healthy diet is essential. First off, the normality of having a healthy breakfast, lunch, or dinner is an act of practicing self-esteem and self-love. Therefore, eating healthy will always boost your self-esteem, lessen emotional issues, and your daily productivity will eventually be taken care of. If you choose to put unhealthy food in your body, you are not protecting the sanctuary that is giving you life. Make a conscious effort tot choose foods that give you the best chance of success, health, and wellness. As we all know, money can't buy health.

6. Be Appreciative More Than You Are Disparaging

Mastering the art of gratitude is a great way to live a happy, stress-free, healthy, and fulfilling life. As French writer Alphonse said: "We can complain because rose plants have thorns or we can rejoice as thorns also have roses." It's always easy to forget how fortunate you are while trying to push through life and the obstacles that come along with it. How do you master this art? Start a journal of appreciation to be grateful for the things you have. Take the time to appreciate those closest to you, those who care about you, and remember at least one good thing about yourself each and every day. Don't forget to make a note of what you have accomplished as well before you go to bed. The more you take notice of the little joys in life, the happier you will be.

7. Be With a Circle of Friends That Are Positive Minded.

Be careful about who you spend your precious time and energy with. A happy life can be contagious if we know where to attract it. Coincidentally, happiness is also the easiest way to develop positivity in our lives. With that in mind, choose to surround yourself which such people who will bring light into your world. Spend time with those who will nurture you each step of the way and don't hesitate to let go of the people who are eating away at your energy and spirits. Let's not forget the wise words of entrepreneur Jim Rohn, "You are the five people you spent the most time averagely. You only live once! Let it be worthwhile.

8. Take Breaks Regularly To Invest in Self-Care.

Although you might be very passionate about your work and your daily schedules, it is okay to take some time - an hour, minute, second, or even a day off. If you take a while to unwind, you will do wonderful things for your mood, mind, and self-esteem. Spend some time doing at least one thing that makes you feel good every day — whether it be listening to music, engaging in sports, starting a new hobby, dabbling in the arts, or even simply preparing a pleasant meal for yourself, you deserve to do it. Whatever floats your boat, don't neglect it!

Conclusion

Determination, persistence, and continuous effort are essential for the development of these habits. It can take just a few weeks or maybe more than a year to develop your habits, so long as you don't stop. It does not matter how long it takes.

What are you waiting for? Pull up your socks; it's your time to win at life.

Chapter 6:

Dealing With Feelings of Overwhelm

Today we're going to talk about a topic that deals with feelings of stress and overwhelm, whether it be from your job or from your family and relationships. I hope that by the end of this video that you will be able to have strategies put in place to help you better cope with the feelings and manage your emotions much better. Hopefully you will also be able to eliminate the things in your life that brings your health into question. My job here is to help you as much as I can so let's begin.

First we have to identify the areas in your life that is bringing you unwanted stress and anxiety. I'm sure that if you think a little harder and dig a little deeper, you will be able to list out the things that are causing you to lose sleep over. The thought of that particular thing would trigger an immediate negative response in your body and only you know what they are.

So lets begin by just brainstorming and listing them down one by one. Take as much time as you need for this exercise. Next I want you to go through your list and arrange them according to which brings the most to the least stress. Now that you have this list, we can talk about the strategies that we can engage in to either reduce or eliminate this overwhelm.

Overwhelm can come from areas in our lives that we feel that we feel are out of control. We feel that we do not have a steady hand or the ability to manage this problem that it manifests into something that suddenly feels too big to handle. It could be something that you dread doing that you have procrastinated on, and that the problem just keeps growing bigger and bigger to the point where you don't even want to touch it. It could be from workloads being piled on top of you one after another by your bosses. It could be a project that you undertook that just maybe is too big for you to handle at your current level and expertise. It could be your family who is giving you additional problems that you have to deal with on top of your workload that is just driving you up the wall. Whatever the stresses are that contributes to your problem, know that they are valid, know that they are real and that they are normal.

Everyone goes through periods of their lives when things just all seem to happen at once. Whether it be having a new baby, a new promotion, a new career, starting a new chapter in life, it is usually those big changes in life that we face overwhelm due to the sudden and added workload that we are not used to. Overwhelm can cause us to lose sleep, lose appetite, gain weight, experience chronic stress, and all these negative aspects can surface in our bodies in ways that affect our health and wellness. When we see these triggers, it is time to make some changes.

We can start by slowing things down a little and carving out time for ourselves to be alone and to recharge. I believe great way for us to get in touch with ourselves is through yoga and meditation. While it might seem like fluff at first, I have personally tried it myself and it is in those moments of calm and relaxation that my head is truly clear. When I am actually able to hear my own thoughts and be aware of what is happening around me. During times we feel overwhelm, things can happen so fast that we lose track of who we are. And sometimes all we need to do is to bring back the attention to ourselves. Find a meditative yoga practice on audible or YouTube, or even Apple Music and Spotify if it is available. Let the teacher guide you through the practice. And just let yourself go for that 30mins or 1 hour that you choose to set aside for yourself. You will be amazed at how calm you will feel and how clear your goals will be if you do it on a regular basis.

With this clarify you may be able to make better decisions that hopefully helps you get through your rough periods that much easier. Whenever you find yourself feeling stress and overwhelm, just give yourself another 15mins to be calm and be guided through a short meditation practice.

The next thing we can do to help alleviate feelings of overwhelm is to practice slow and deep breathing. Focusing on the breath as been proven to reduce stress by triggering a physiological response in our body. We trick our brain into slowing down and focusing on one thing and one thing only. This trick can help to calm you in moments of deep anxiety when you feel the world is crashing down on you and you are not sure what to do. Just sit still for a moment and engage in this practice.

Now we have to address the elephant in the room which is what are the areas in your life that are triggering these responses from your body that is causing you to feel overwhelm. And is there any way we can eliminate these stressors from your life. Again as I have said many times before, if this thing you are doing is bringing you such immense dread and overwhelm, maybe it is time you simply walk away from it forever if that is an option. You have to ask yourself if what you are doing can justify putting your mental and physical state in jeopardy. Whether maybe the money is worth risking your health over, or whether this person is worth keeping in your life if he or she brings you much anguish. I always believe that life is too short to be filled with things that overwhelm us. A little stress is good for us but chronic and prolonged periods of exposure to this can in fact cause us to die sooner. As cortisol is constantly being pumped into your bloodstream it can have serious negative consequences for our physical health, not to mention our mental health in the form of depression.

Sometimes we have to tell ourselves it is okay to simply walk away when we have no other option. Something or someone else will turn up that is better for us if we put ourselves first.

So I urge all of you to take a hard look at the list you have created today. Which ones on those list have you been suffering for prolonged periods of time with seemingly no end to it? Could you eliminate it from your life or take a smaller role on it? Always remember that you are what you take on, and that you have the power to decide what you want in your life. I believe you know how to make the right decisions for yourself as well.

Don't Be Demotivated By Fear

What are you doing right now? What ambitions do you have for the morning to come? What doubts you have in mind? What is stopping you right now?

You have doubts about anything because you want to be cautious. You are hesitant because you have your gut telling you to think again. The reality is you are afraid and you don't know it. Or maybe you do know it but you keep ignoring your weakness.

That weakness you keep ignoring is your fear. Fear starts with a seed but if left alone can manifest deeper roots and can have a devastating impact on one's personality.

Fear is the biggest enemy of commitment. Fear kills productivity. Fear eats creativity. Fear crushes motivation.

People keep fears as if they are being smart about unexpected outcomes. You don't need to stay afraid of things to abstain from them. The only thing you need to fear is the 'Fear' itself.

When you were a child, your parents motivated you and gave you the confidence to get over most of your fears. But now you would be considered stupid and childish if you seek a mentor. You what do you do?

The answer is simple. You have yourself to try out things that make you take a step back. Because fear is self-imposed. You made yourself prone to such feelings and you can make them go away as well.

Fear can make you second guess your own abilities.

We are way behind our goals because subconsciously we have thought of the failure that can happen. The fear of our dreams shattering overtakes the ambition and happiness when you finally get to the scale. This overburdening feeling of fear keeps us sitting in our seats and stops us from trying out new things. This fear makes us believe that we don't deserve what we have dreamt of.

So I have a question for you! What have you done in the last week, or month or even a year to overcome only the smallest phobia?

If you haven't, it is possible that you won't leave what you have right now and never go for anything more than you can own. This reason is that fear makes you remain content with whatever nature and God have bestowed upon you on time after time. But you won't get up and try to work new things for bigger and better blessings that hard work and some gutsy calls have to offer.

If you can't give up the feeling of harm that might come if you finally decide to indulge in those reluctant goals, take a different approach then. Think of it as what can you be on that other side of the river? What colors does the other side of the canvas have? What laughs can you have if you made that one joke? What gains you can have if you increased just one pound?

If you try to make your fears a medium of self-analysis, maybe you start to gain the motivation that faded quickly with every second you spent in front of that source of fear. Then you might start to see a whole new image of your personality and this might be the person you always wish you could be!

Chapter 7:

7 Ways To Remove Excess Noise In Your Life

Ever felt lost in a world that is so fast-paced, where no two moments are the same? Do you ever have a hard time achieving your goals, just because you have more distractions than a purpose to jump to success?

We live in a time, where technology is the biggest ease as well as the biggest difficulty while achieving our goals.

When you need something to be fixed, the internet can save us a lot of time, but the same internet can prove to be the biggest cause to take away the focus of the most determined too.

Although there are many important things on the internet too, that are essential to our daily lives, we don't need them at all times. Especially the realm of social media platforms.

Youtube, Facebook even Instagram can prove to be a beneficial tool for learning and teaching. But it can also make you spend more and more time on things that won't give you much except a good laugh here and there.

So what habits or activities can you adapt to distill these distractions. Reduce noise in life helping you focus better on the things that matter the most.

1. Divide your Tasks Into Smaller Ones

When you already have many distractions in life, including the household tasks and other daily life chores that you must attend to, then you must not avoid those.

But your dreams and goals must not be put aside at all, instead one must learn to complete them by dividing them into smaller, more manageable tasks.

Those who depend on you must have you when they need you, but that shouldn't stop you from doing what you require from yourself.

That can be done by keeping your head in the work whenever you get the chance to get maximum results from those short intervals.

2. Manage Your Time Smartly

Life is too short to be indulging in every whim and activity that you crave. Not everything or thought requires you to act upon.

A human being is the smartest being on this planet but also the stupidest. When a man or a woman wants to achieve something with all their heart, they do get it eventually. But when they have a thousand silly desires to go for, they slide off the set path as if there were none.

"You only Live Once".

Logically, this is a valid quote to get anyone off their path to success. But, realistically this is also the most common reason for the failure of a majority of our youngsters.

You only get this life once, So you must go for the acts that bring you a better future with a surety of freedom without having to rely on anyone. Life doesn't need to be a continuous struggle once you use your energies at the right time for the right time.

3. Get Your Head Out of Social Media

I know this may sound a little Grownup and cliched, but we spend more time on our mobiles and laptops than going out and doing something physically in all our senses with our actual hands.

We can believe and act on anything that pops up on this screen but rarely do we get anything worthwhile that we can adapt to change our lives once and for all.

Social media might be the new medium and source of knowledge and business for many, but for a layman, this is also the biggest waste of creative energy.

There is a lot out there to do in real life, a lot that we can realistically achieve. But, these days, we tend to hide behind a simple tweet and believe that we have done enough when the reality could have been much different.

4. Avoid Unhealthy Relationships

You might have always heard that a friend can be an emotional escape when you need one, but the excess of friends can prove to be the opposite of that. People seem to think, the more friends you have, the better you have a chance to stay engaged and have a happy social life. But this isn't always the case.

The more you have friends, your devotion gets scattered and you find solace in everyone's company. This makes you more exposed, and people might take advantage of that. The fewer friends you have, the better loyalty you can expect and better returns of a favor.

When you have fewer friends, even if you lose one someday or get deceived, you would require less time to bounce back from the incident and you won't have to worry for long.

5. Get Out of Home Environment

Productivity required a productive environment. People tend to look for ease, but it doesn't always help us with finding our true potential.

You sometimes need a strict office environment or a more organized station or workplace. A place where there is no distraction or source of wandering thoughts to get your attention.

People need to understand how our brains work. If you cannot focus sitting in your bed, get a chair and a table. If that doesn't work for you, take a stool without a backrest. If you still feel at ease, just pick a standing table and start working while standing on your feet.

This makes your mind stay more focused on the task at hand to be done quickly.

6. Make A Schedule For These Distractions

If you feel like you can't give up the urge to pick your phone and check your feed. Or if you need to watch the last quarter of the league, Or if you need to have a smoke.

Don't start fighting these urges. It won't help you, rather make things worse.

If you cannot let go off of these things, it's fine. Make a deal with your brain, that you need this last page done within the next 10 minutes, and then I can go do what I needed direly.

You have to come at peace with your mind and work as a single unit. So make time for these distractions and gradually you might be able to drop them once and for all.

7. You Don't Have to Compare With Anyone

Why do we humans need to compare and compete? Because we think it keeps our drive and our struggle alive. We think it gives us a reason and a purpose to go on and makes us see our goals more clearly.

Comparing to others won't make you see 'Your Goals', rather you would start creating goals that were never meant to be for you. You have these priorities just because you saw someone with something that appealed to you.

This is the noise and distraction that deviates you from the path that was meant to be for you all along.

If you want a clear vision of what you want, start removing cluttered thoughts, acts, and people from your life. It might seem hard at the start, but you won't have any regrets once everything comes in place.

Chapter 8:

6 Ways On How To Change Your Body Language To Attract Success

"If you want to find the truth, do not listen to the words coming to you. Rather see the body language of the speaker. It speaks the facts not audible." - Bhavesh Chhatbar.

Our body language is exceptionally essential as 60-90% of our communication with others is nonverbal. If properly used, it can be our key to more tremendous success. We focus more on our business plans, our marketing drives, and our spreadsheets rather than considering our facial expressions, posture, or what our physical gestures might be saying about us. Our mindset also plays a role in how our body language expresses itself. No matter how impressive our words maybe, if we are sending a negative signal with our body language, we would eventually lose the opportunities of gaining more success.

Here is a list to help you change your body language to attract more success.

1. The Power of Voice

Your personal voice has a huge impact and can literally make or break your success. It is one of the most direct routes to empower your communication. The pitch of your voice, its timbre, cadence, volume, and the speed with which you speak, are all influential factors that will ensure how convincing you are and how people will judge your character. Lowering your voice at the right moment or injecting some spontaneity into it when needed will enhance your credibility and lend you an air of intelligence. We must fill our voices with our range and depth if we want others and ourselves to take us seriously.

2.   The Power of Listening

An excellent speaking skill represents only half of the leadership expression. The other half is mastering your art in listening. While a good listener is incredibly rare, it is essential to keep our ears open to any valuable information that is often silently transmitted. When we start listening attentively to others, we begin to notice what a person is saying and decode accurately what they don't say. You will also begin to realize what the other person is thinking or whether their attitude is positive or hostile towards you. With these particular observations, you will likely attune to another person and create the bond crucial to a successful working life.

3.   The Necessity for Emotional Intelligence

The skill of acute listening develops our emotional intelligence, the intuition to ascertain the objective reality of the situation. When we lack emotional intelligence, we might misinterpret situations and fail to decipher what might be needed. Emotional intelligence deepens our empathy. It gives us the ability to be present and listen to someone when they need it the most. It is the single best predictor of performance in the workplace and can be the most vital driver of personal excellence and leadership. Our understanding of emotional intelligence will vastly improve our internal relations and can also deepen our sense of personal fulfillment and professional accomplishment.

4. The Power of Eye Contact

Making eye contact and holding it is seen as a sign of confidence, and the other person is felt valued. It increases your chance of being trustful and respected as they tend to listen to you more attentively and feel comfortable giving you their insights. You may be shy, an introvert, or might have heard that it's impolite to maintain eye contact with a superior. But in many parts of the world, business people expect you to maintain eye contact 50-60% of the time. Here's a simple tip: when you meet someone, look into their eyes long enough to notice their eye color.

5. Talk With Your Hands

There's a region in our brain called the Broca's area, which is essential and active during our speech production and when we wave our hands. Gestures are integrally linked to speech, so gesturing while talking can speed up your thinking. Using hand gestures while talking can improve verbal content as well as make your speechless hesitant. You will see that it will help you form clearer thoughts with more declarative language and speak in tighter sentences.

6. Strike A Power Pose

Research conducted at Harvard and Columbia Business Schools into the effects of body posture and confidence show that holding your body in expansive high-power poses (such as leaning back with hands behind the head or standing with legs and arms stretched wide open) for only as little as two minutes can stimulate high levels of testosterone (a hormone linked to power) and lower levels of cortisol (a stress hormone). You will look and feel more confident and inevitable, leading to an increased feeling of energy and a high tolerance for risk.

Conclusion

Most of our body language and movement are subconscious, so it can be challenging to retrain ourselves away from habits we have had for years. Still, we must try to master our body language, too, with the art of public speaking. Regular practice Is the key to success and the quickest route to attain confident body language as with any other skill. Practice them in your day-to-day life so that they may become deep-rooted. Be less compliant and step into an edgier, emboldened, and more genuine you.

Chapter 9:

7 Habits To Do Everyday

In the words of Aristotle, *we are what we repeatedly do. Excellence then is not an act, but a habit.* An act that we repeat eventually becomes ingrained in us; it forms part of our culture and lifestyle. We speak, think and act out of the abundance of our hearts.

Here are 7 habits to do every day:

1. Praying

You have heard of the saying that an apple a day keeps the doctor away; but I dare pose to you, a prayer a day keeps the devil away. Praying is not an act for the religious or spiritual. Regardless of your faith, prayer is a pop-up notification in our lives that cannot be put off no matter how often we snooze it.

It has nothing to do with divinity but the humanity in us. Only in prayer can we be vulnerable without fear of it being used against us. We surrender our mortality to the immortal one. Prayer psyches our morale and gives us the confidence to face the uncertainty of tomorrow.

Before talking to mortals, talk to the supernatural in prayer. In solitude, you can only do so much. Prayer provides the much-needed avenue to vent to someone at the other end of the line – God.

2. Reading

Great leaders are readers (read that again). Reading widens our knowledge base and we stay up to date in current affairs. Being among the wisest of his generation, Haile Selassie says *A man who says "I have learned enough and will learn no further" should be considered as knowing nothing at all.*

Knowledge is power. Amass yourself as much of it as possible. Read newspapers and lifestyle magazines to catch up with the fast-moving world, read inspirational and motivational blogs and articles to be inspired to dream bigger, and read business magazines to be at par with innovations that will blow up your mind.

Reading gives you immeasurable exposure. Challenge yourself to read at least two books (even e-books) in one month and watch yourself grow.

3. Cleaning

Cleanliness is next to godliness. It is supposed to be a routine activity, not one to be scheduled to be done on particular days only. There is this misconception, especially in Africa, that cleaning is a gender role. No, it is not. It is everyone's responsibility to keep their immediate environment clean and not delegate it to another person, for there is only so much that they can do.

Most people fail at this because they keep postponing cleaning duties. Why do it later when you can do it now? Do your laundry, wash your utensils, clean your kitchen, take shower, dust off your working space at the office, routinely dust off your laptop or desktop, get a clean shave (for the gents) every so often to maintain your facial hair too, and even dust off seats before you sit down. Do not wait for someone else to take responsibility for your cleanliness. It is a sign of irresponsibility on your part.

Cleanliness has immense benefits. Do you remember how you felt after taking that warm bath at the end of your busy day? How well were you received at your workstation when you showed up clean-shaven and well-groomed? Embracing cleanliness will open doors that character alone cannot.

4. Being Kind

A person's character is known from how they treat strangers, hotel attendants, public service vehicle operators, the needy in the streets, and those who have no means to repay them. Kindness is a habit, not an occasional act.

Make a point of being kind to those you meet every day. Do to others what you would like to be done to you. Karma is there to equalize the math. Kindness has no affiliation with being religious (although it is a doctrine in religion), but it is about being a better person. If you can donate to that charity event, do it generously. If you can clear the hospital bill of the sick, do it willingly. If you can pay fees for the needy students, kindly step in.

Make kindness your habit and generosity a part of you. It is not to mean that you become irrationally kind. Use rational judgment to distinguish between genuine and fake needy people. A simple act of kindness will change someone's life.

5. Planning

If you fail to plan, you are planning to fail. Planning arises from simple ignorable things. The not-so-petty matters that we overlook and comfort ourselves by saying it will not happen again. How often have we done impulse buying when shopping? It may look trivial but its impact on our finances cannot be overlooked.

Get your acts together and prioritize planning. Earn before you spend and save after you earn. Failure to plan will drive you to bankruptcy and depression. A good plan is a job half done. When you anticipate what will come next, you will be prepared to handle it effectively. That is what planning does to a man. It makes you a semi-god with the ability to come up with solutions to problems that are yet to come but are around the corner.

Isn't it adorable how powerful planning is? It is neither tedious as many see it nor reserved for the elite. A plan is essential for personal success.

6.   Learn Something New

Knowledge is power. The best gift you can give yourself is to widen your knowledge base. Learn life hacks, human psychology and socializing. There are those lessons which cannot be taken in a classroom but out there in the real world. Take it upon yourself to learn something new daily.

Nothing is stagnant in the current world. Walk with the changes lest you be left behind. Adapt to new practices in your industry fast enough before most people do. Your flexibility will bring something to the table and you will attract greatness.

Learning something new daily is not solely academic. Regardless of your level of education, there is always something to learn. Do not despise those below you in the social ladder, you can always learn a thing or two.

7. Talk To At Least One Stranger

We all are reluctant to talk to strangers for one reason or another. We are worried about how they will respond to our greetings or maybe our proposals. One thing however is clear – strangers could be the potential turning point of our businesses and jobs. They could be the breakthrough we have been waiting for.

Pick up the courage to greet a stranger today and further a conversation. Be warned that some could be opportunists and exploit your goodwill. Nevertheless, talk to a stranger. Greet the people you find at the bus stage and the security guard at your place.

These 7 habits to do everyday are essential for personal growth.

Chapter 10:

10 Habits of Bernard Arnault

Bernard Arnault- French investor, businessman, and CEO of LVMH recently reclaimed the title "worlds' wealthiest" from fellow billionaire Jeff Bezos. His business acumen and awe-inspiring financial achievements deserve to be recognized. His perspective can serve as a model for entrepreneurs who want to follow in his footsteps.

Bernard Arnault has written about money, prosperity, leadership, and power over the years. Moreover, his path to becoming the CEO of one of the world's most recognized brands will provide you with valuable lessons to emulate from. That is, your life circumstances shouldn't stop you from expanding and thriving outside your expertise.

Following his impressive accomplishments, here are ten points you can take away from Arnault's journey to success.

1. Happiness Before Money

According to Bernard, happiness is leading. That is leading your team to the top whether you are in business, sports, music industry. Money, according to him, is a consequence, and success is a blend of your past and future.

Your priority is not what you'll make sooner! When you put much-required effort into your job, profits will flow.

2. Mistakes Your Lesson

Your biggest mistake is your learning opportunity. When your business isn't performing well, understand the situation first and be patient.

In the world of innovative brands, it can take years to get something to work. Give it time and put yourself in a long-term expectation.

3. Always Behave as a Startup

Think small. Act quickly. Smaller boats can turn faster than more giant tankers. Arnault emphasizes the significance of thinking small. LVMH, in Arnault's opinion, is not a massive corporation device with miles of unnecessary bureaucracy.

Believe in your vision while attracting the best talent for your success path. A handy, adaptable speed, one that can fail quickly as easy to sleeve up.

4. Continuously Reinvent Yourself

How do you maintain your relevance? Bernard's LVMH is built on innovation, quality, entrepreneurship, and, essentially, on long-term vision. LVMH excels at developing increasingly desirable new products and selling them globally.

To be successful today, with your capabilities, opt for a worldwide startup and see what's going on. This necessitates a more considerable investment, which gives you an advantage. However, let the Creators run your inventions.

5. Team-Creative Control

Arnault strategies find creative control under each product's team to do what they do best. Arnault's designers are the dreamer's realists and critics. Allow your team to take creative control. You risk putting a tourniquet around their minds if you restrict them in any way.

6. Create Value To Attract Customers

Marketing investigates what the customer desires. As a result, you are doing what they need: creating a product and testing it to see if it works. Keeping your products in close contact with consumers, according to Arnault, makes a desire to buy in them. LVMH creates products that generate customers. For him, it's never about sales; it's always about creating desire. Your goal should be to be desirable for long-term marketability.

7. Trust the Process

There will always be different voices in business, and while there will undoubtedly be good advice, if you believe an idea will succeed, you may need to persevere until the end. Like Arnault, disregard your critics by following through with your vision to excel.

8. Your Persistence Is Everything

It would be best if you were very persistent. It would be best to have ideas, but the idea is only 20% of the equation. The execution rate is 80%. So if you are trying out a startup, having ideas marvellous, the driving force is persistence and execution.

When it comes to the most successful startups, such as Facebook, the idea was great from the beginning. Others, however, had the same idea. So why is Facebook such a phenomenal success today? It is critically through execution with persistence.

9. Do Not Think of Yourself

Bernard Arnault can be differentiated from other billionaires like Elon Musk or Bill Gates by focusing on the brands, making their longevity rather than making himself the face. He is only concerned with promoting his products.

To accomplish this, you must maintain contact with pioneers and designers, for example, while also making their ideas more specific and sustainable.

10. Maintain Contact With Your Company

One of the most common leadership mistakes is to lose sight of the company once you reach the top and "stick" with manageable goals. Instead, to see if the machine is working correctly or if there is room for improvement, you must examine every corner and every part of it.

Conclusion

Your willingness to outwork and your ability to outlearn everyone will keep your success journey intact and going. Bernard Arnault's path to becoming the CEO of the worlds most recognized and desired multibillion empire of brands have a valuable lesson for you: your starting point does not influence or determine your future destination.